What a difference a year makes

A heartwarming story of my transplant journey

By
Lianne Derbyshire

Contents

Preface

I decided to write this book as a memory of what I've been through but also in the hope it'll help others going through a similar experience.

I never thought I'd have to have a heart transplant, and it was a scary time. This book shows the ups and downs of what happened to me.

I'm sure everyone's experience is different. But if you or a family member or friend are like me. With no previous heart problems, then this may help you to understand some of what's happening or about to happen.

How it all began

I'll start by introducing myself. I've been married to Peter for 23 years. We have two boys - Jack (22) and Tom (15). I was always very fit and healthy but Christmas 2018, when I was 46 years old, I started to feel unwell. Headache, achy all over, tight chest and generally exhausted.

My sister Diane and nephew Ian were both ill, too. Christmas Day was a bit of a disaster. I managed to cook the dinner, everything went perfectly – all cooked at the right time - but we sat down to eat and I just couldn't face it. I began to feel sick. I just sat there. I didn't want to ruin it for the rest of my family. Diane didn't eat much either.

As the days went on, things didn't really improve. Eventually Peter said he thought I should go to the doctors. I did and was prescribed antibiotics. Diane and Ian braved it and, although it took a long time until they started feeling better, whatever it was did eventually clear on its own.

The antibiotics worked for me. I felt better after a week. Luckily, I was working from home, so hadn't had to take any time off sick.

I felt good for a couple of weeks, things were pretty much back to normal. Then, gradually, things changed. I started to get out of breath even just walking up the stairs. If I carried the clean washing upstairs, I'd have to sit on the bed to get my breath back.

I tried to carry on. I had no appetite but managed to eat small amounts.

One day, I had to go into the office to print off some work. I boxed it up and left with it at about 7pm. The 5 minute walk to the car park was the longest ever. The box was heavy and at one point I didn't think I would make it to my car. I stopped at the railings of the car park, but forced myself to carry on. I eventually got to the car, opened the boot and threw the box in. I sat in the car completely out of breath, feeling sick, and had to wait a few minutes before even attempting to drive.

As the days went on, I was eating less and less, but my weight seemed to be increasing. I was feeling worse. A weird feeling in my stomach, breathlessness. When I breathed in, I felt like I wasn't getting enough oxygen, so I made an appointment at the doctors. I explained what my symptoms were and was prescribed Irritable Bowel Syndrome medication to see if that helped. It didn't.

By now my ankles had started to swell. I kept a diary of my weight and every day it increased even though I was hardly eating anything. If I did eat anything I'd have to go to the toilet and vulgar as it sounds, I felt I had to be sick or open my bowels for some kind of relief. I was also having problems sleeping. I couldn't lie flat anymore - I had to prop myself up. Things were getting worse, so I made another appointment at the doctors. I'd done it online and hadn't realised I'd made the appointment with a nurse. I was called in and I explained my symptoms.

The nurse said there was nothing she could do; I'd need to see a doctor. I burst into tears. Luckily, she said that if I waited, she would get me an appointment, but I'd have to go and sit back in the waiting room. I asked if I could have a few minutes to compose myself. I calmed myself down, then went back to the waiting room.

Not long after, I was called in to see the doctor. I explained everything that'd happened, my previous visit and being prescribed IBS medication. I told her about my increasing weight gain, the breathlessness and what happened when I breathed in. The feeling in my stomach and the fact that I needed to get some relief if I did manage to eat anything. And I showed her my ankles.

She said she would arrange for some tests to be done. She wrote down blood tests and an ECG on a piece of paper. She told me to go back to reception and hand them the piece of paper; they'd make the appointment for me. I did and was given an appointment for two weeks' time.

I went home and again tried to carry on as normal, but I did call my office and tell them I wouldn't be in as I felt so bad.

The next week I tried to work from home again, I was only in the Monday as it was Peter's Birthday on the Tuesday and I'd already booked that off. Tuesday came and Peter knew how I was feeling, but I didn't want to ruin his birthday, so I insisted we go out somewhere.

The weather wasn't great, so we decided to go to a shopping mall. He'd got some birthday money, so he might spot something that he wanted to buy. How I walked round there, I don't know. But I think Peter could tell it wasn't easy, so we didn't stay very long.

The afternoon came and went, and I really didn't think I could go out for a meal. The kids loved pizza, so we got a takeaway. I managed to eat one slice and then as usual for me at the time, just put my feet up on the sofa and tried to relax. I was feeling really rough, it got to about 10pm and I was in the bathroom. I felt I needed to be sick, which I was. But this time there appeared to be blood in it.

I shouted to Peter who said he was taking me to our local hospital in Tameside. There's a car park very close to the A&E department so we parked up and then slowly walked to the entrance.

I explained to the receptionist what the problem was. And then sat in the waiting area. I was called to be triaged by a nurse. After hearing my symptoms, she ran an ECG test. I then sat back in the waiting area. Not long after, I was called in to see a doctor. While I was waiting, I began to feel sick, so I was given a sick bowl. The doctor came and listened to what I had to say and reviewed my test results. He said the ECG had shown a slight abnormality but nothing too concerning. By now it was about 2am. He said he'd make me an appointment for the next day. He said to go to the Ambulatory department for lunchtime. Peter and I left the hospital. While walking back to the car park I was sick again. And again, there was blood in it. We got home and tried to get some sleep.

The next day we arrived back at the hospital. We parked in a different car park which was closer to the Outpatients department. But the walk to the entrance was about 5 minutes and uphill. We had to stop halfway as I just couldn't breathe. I nearly cried, but managed to stop myself. Eventually we arrived at the right department. It was quite busy, but I was assessed and then asked to go for a chest x-ray. When I came back the nurse explained that there was a shadow on my lungs, possible pneumonia. She said I would be admitted. I was put on IVR antibiotics which made me feel very sick, so the nurse gave me some anti-sickness drugs. They made me feel very dizzy, as though I could fall off the bed. Peter nipped home to get some things for me, but told the nurse on his way out about how I was feeling.

When Peter got back, we asked the nurse what was happening, thinking she'd give us an update about how they'd treat the pneumonia. But she said they were more concerned about the size of my heart.

She mentioned it being 5 times the size that it should be, and I remember her talking about heart failure. I messaged my sisters, Diane and Debbie, and told them what the nurse had said. We all thought that was crazy and that it couldn't be heart failure.

I was moved to a ward for the first night. I didn't get much sleep, even though there were very few patients, so it wasn't noisy. But the sickness continued and again there was blood in it. The nurses didn't seem very concerned, but it was quite scary for me.

The next day I was moved to another ward with lots of other patients. All had different problems, and most were a lot older than me. I was still being given antibiotics which were making me really sick, so again I was given anti-sickness drugs. Sometimes these were given orally and sometimes intravenously.

I couldn't eat a thing, despite my family telling me I needed to build my strength up. I lost a lot of weight – well over a stone - but my ankles were still quite swollen. I had quite a few visitors, family and friends, but I wasn't really 'with it'. Thinking about it now, I wished someone had taken a photograph of me then, as apparently I looked like I was at death's door. I'd like to see how bad I really looked and compare it to today.

I was allowed to get out of bed and use the bathroom, which I did manage to do. On one occasion after having the intravenous anti-sickness drugs I was convinced I'd driven home from the hospital.

I knew Peter had gone to the Manchester City football match so I text my son Tom, to come downstairs. I also messaged Diane asking her to bring me back to the hospital. They both ignored me! I've since found out that Diane did ring the hospital to check I was ok. I also apparently text Peter who left the match early to come and see me.

I was on that ward for a few more days but didn't seem to be improving. Then one night a bed became available for me on the Coronary Care Unit, so I was moved. Peter stayed while I settled in. Then later that night after he'd gone, I was told they were going to perform a procedure to put a line into my neck.

I was told it was quite a complex procedure and I think I had to give consent for it to be done. I just remember lots of doctors appearing and me being lay down completely flat, which was really uncomfortable for me then. They did what they needed to do and then put a dressing on.

I was hooked up to lots of medication intravenously. I was able to eat a bit by now. But was only able to get out of bed to sit in a chair with the help of the nurses. I was given bed baths, had to use a commode and also had a catheter. I'd never imagined that at 46, this is what I'd have to do.

I had a few visitors as the days went by. My niece Cheryl from Preston brought her family. My sister Debbie came from Bristol with all her family. And I had visits from a few friends, too.

The nurses were all so lovely, and I quickly got into the routine. Waking up for breakfast which was brought on a trolley and you decided what you wanted from cereals, toast, tea, coffee, etc. Next it was wash time and then I was moved to the chair.

There was lots of talk about moving me to another hospital, one that specialised in heart problems. Wythenshawe was the closest, but they didn't have any spare beds. Also mentioned were Birmingham, Newcastle and London. The favourite appeared to be the Queen Elizabeth Hospital in Birmingham; this looked like the first to possibly have a free bed. Every day the nurses rang round to see if there was a bed available for me.

One morning the doctors were doing their rounds and a senior doctor came to see me. I was all alone and he asked if I knew why I was being moved. I replied saying "To get better". He said, in a very matter of fact tone, "No, you need a new heart, or you won't survive". After he'd gone I cried. I didn't realise things were that bad. A nurse calmed me down.

I stayed on that ward for a further 2 weeks. It'd now been 3 weeks since I was admitted, and I hadn't been able to have a shower. I've never not washed my hair for that long!

Transfer to the Queen Elizabeth Hospital, Birmingham

The call came through that there was a bed in Birmingham for me. I was strapped to a bed that would be taken in the ambulance. A nurse and an anaesthetist came with me in the ambulance. We were blue lighted all the way to Birmingham. The anaesthetist started to feel sick in the back of the ambulance. It was a very small place for the 3 of us and a paramedic. The windows were opened to let some air in.

I arrived at Birmingham and was wheeled to the Coronary Care Unit. It was a strange ward, circular in shape; beds all around. They made me feel very welcome, though. I was swabbed for MRSA and the handover was done. When the nurse and anaesthetist left, I felt very alone. I had no service on my phone so the nurse lent me the ward phone so I could call Peter to let him know where I was.

Peter came to visit me. He was amazed at the size of the hospital. I think it had taken him about 2 and a half hours to get there. A journey he made so many times over the next 6 weeks.

I was still hooked up to lots of medication, so still no shower for me. The doctors visited me and explained that they'd be doing lots of tests. The impression I got was that I might not need a new heart after all.

Maybe there was something they could do for me that didn't involve having to have a heart transplant. A test was scheduled for the next day, but you never knew what time you'd be called.

Dinner arrived so I asked the nurse if I was ok to eat it. I was told that I could, but then half an hour later I was told that the test couldn't go ahead. I was upset and asked if it was because I'd eaten my lunch. I was assured that that wasn't the reason. I just wanted to do what was right, not be a burden, so it upset me that maybe I'd jeopardised having the test that I needed.

Later that afternoon, I was told that the test was going to go ahead after all. I was wheeled out of the ward and taken to the Cath Lab. It resembled an operating theatre and was very cold. The nurses helped me transfer to the bed that was in there. They asked if I wanted a blanket, to which I said yes.

The blankets were kept in a warm room so it was really nice to have that placed on top of me. The procedure, which thinking back now must have been my first biopsy, involved placing a needle in my neck – the jugular vein. Because this is quite dangerous, I was connected to an ECG machine and my blood pressure was taken regularly throughout to make sure I was doing ok.

First some anaesthetic was used to numb my neck area. Then, after a few minutes, something was inserted into my neck and I felt lots of pushing and pulling. I'd closed my eyes because I was a little scared about what I might see. But if I'd have had my eyes open (I realised this on subsequent biopsies), I'd have seen the screen to my left which showed whatever it was going down into my body – like an x-ray kind of thing.

I don't know what the doctors thought, me keeping my eyes closed. Because after the procedure the doctor was speaking to me and I was lying there with my eyes closed. Eventually I realised I should open them. I must've looked so daft! I was then taken back to the ward.

As the time went on, it began to get really painful. The dressing that was put on my neck felt really tight. It was like my throat was closing up, so I asked for some pain killers.

The next day I was told I was being moved to a single ward as the swabs I'd had taken when I arrived had shown I had MRSA. It was lovely to be given a single room. It didn't have a bathroom though, so I had to use a commode again. And I did feel a bit like I had the plague. Signs were put up outside my door warning people that they needed to take extra precautions when entering and leaving the room.

A commode was left in my room permanently, so I had to ring my bell when I'd used it so it could be emptied. One of the medications I was on, was to try and get the fluid off my lungs so I did have to urinate quite regularly. And because I was connected to several drips which were on a stand, I had to wheel that with me every time I went on the commode. I didn't like pressing my bell in the middle of the night, as it'd wake the other patients up.

There was one awful incident, where I'd just assumed a bed pan had been replaced in the commode the last time it was emptied. I did both, if you know what I mean. I was mortified! There was no way I could've cleaned up the mess myself, properly. So, I had no choice but to call the nurse. She was so lovely, I'm sure it's happened before but I just kept apologising over and over again. I never made that mistake again!

I stayed on this ward about 2 weeks in total. I had lots of visitors. Debbie and her family, Peter's Dad Stewart and his wife Shirley who visited me every Thursday. Cheryl and her daughter Melody, and lots of other family. Also friends from work which was lovely especially considering how far away from home I was. But in the back of my mind was the thought that they were all coming to say goodbye. And I couldn't hug anyone as they left as I had to try my best not to pick up any germs.

I'd set up a group chat on Messenger with lots of family and friends so I could update them on what was happening. This turned out to be a great 'pick me up' for me. I'd get messages each morning, letting me know what everyone was up to. And then each night wishing me a restful night's sleep. I also received phone calls from friends, which was so lovely to know that they were thinking of me.

I had daily visits from the doctors. The tests that I'd had so far proved that I did need a new heart. But just because you need one, doesn't mean you can be added to the transplant list. How sad is that? I needed further tests to check that the rest of my organs were working as they should. The doctors needed to make sure I was healthy enough to have a transplant.

There was another option, a Left Ventricular Assist Device could be fitted. This would be connected to my existing heart, it's like a battery pack, worn outside the body. If you had one of those, you could no longer swim or have a bath. You could shower, so long as it was completely covered up. I really didn't want that; I really hoped that I could be added to the transplant list.

All I could think about was my Mum. She died when she was 49. I was only 19 at the time. She got cancer and because she was diagnosed so late, she was told there was nothing that could be done for her.

11

Her diagnosis was in the December and she passed away the following April. I was 46 now, would the same apply to me or would I be lucky enough to be placed on the transplant list?

I continued on the medication, but because I still had fluid on my lungs the doctors decided to restrict the amount of liquids I drank. I was thirsty, but I had to work out how much water I needed each day to take my tablets. So, with my meals I could only drink a very small amount. And when the tea trolley came round, I had to say no.

I'd always sorted out the finances at home, Peter was trying to keep working, keep things running at home and visit me. I felt ok so asked him to bring everything in on his next visit so I could keep on top of those. I also had lots of magazines and word searches that kept me going and passed the time. I had lots of food to eat, and my little cupboard was full of goodies that my visitors had been bringing me. I needed to put the weight back on that I'd lost. It was hard, believe it or not. On top of my normal meals, I was given protein shakes that I had to drink to get my weight up as quickly as possible. So, I'd tend to eat the goodies from my cupboard in an evening.

The doctors visited me one day as usual but had some fantastic news for me. The tests I'd had, had shown that the rest of my organs were working fine. They were going to place me on the transplant list.

There were 3 lists:

Emergency, meaning you're in hospital on life support.

Urgent, you're in hospital; too ill to be sent home.

Standard, you need a transplant but can go home to wait until a heart becomes available.

A meeting was arranged with my family and one of the transplant nurses, Brian. Brian explained what would happen and then asked if we had any questions. Did you know, only about 200 heart transplants are done in the UK each year? I didn't.

Peter was at the meeting along with Diane, Debbie, Peter's mum Jean and her husband Rhys, who'd both travelled all the way from France. I remember being pleased that everyone was there to listen to Brian; they might remember things he'd said that I didn't.

But everyone was asking questions. I just sat there, in the corner thinking 'I've got things to ask', but it was difficult as everyone else had so much to ask as well.

I was given booklets to read and forms to fill in. I had to make a choice about the heart I'd hopefully receive. There were lots of options. For example, I had to decide if I would accept the heart of an over 60-year-old, or a heart of someone who had taken drugs in the past etc. There were about 5 things I had to consider.

I ticked that I would accept any heart. I came to the conclusion, after speaking with my family, that it could mean I'd get a heart quicker than if I was choosy. After all, the doctors would check the heart fully when it became available, to make sure it looked ok and would be ok to be used. I also had to fill in a consent form.

A transplant nurse visited me late one Friday night, she said she was just popping in to say hello and to see how I was feeling. I didn't think anything of it, but I don't know now if it was because tomorrow was going to be a big day!

Transplant Day

I'll never forget the next day. I was woken up at 6:15 by the same transplant nurse who'd visited me the night before. To say I was surprised was an understatement. She asked if I remembered her, and I said I did. She then went on to tell me that there may be a new heart for me. I'd only been on the transplant list for 4 days!

The transplant nurse said my family were waiting outside my room. They'd been called in the early hours and asked to make their way to the hospital. I was in shock, I burst into tears when my family came in. We were all warned that the new heart needed to be fully checked, before we'd know if it was ok to be used.

I had to prepare though, ready. This meant nothing to eat or drink, having a wash and making sure my groin area was clean shaven. They sometimes need to access this area during the operation. The time went slowly, with lots of nervous conversations. Then, at about 10am, I was told that the operation would be going ahead. The porters came in and wheeled me down the corridor to the operating theatre.

My family came with me. Saying my goodbyes was one of the hardest things I've ever had to do. The thought that I may not wake up, and never see my family again, was heart-breaking. I'm not sure how my family coped. I know every operation involves risks, but this was major. I was terrified.

I was wheeled into the pre-op area. It was a very small room, I had lots of needles inserted into my arms.

One was to take my blood pressure during the operation, apparently. Then a mask was placed over my face; within seconds I was asleep. My family went back to my ward to collect my things and take them home. I'd be going straight to the Intensive Care Unit after the operation so there'd be no room for my belongings.

The operation lasted 5 hours. Peter was called by the transplant team about halfway through, to say that my new heart had been inserted, but not connected up at that point. They told him that everything seemed to be going well.

I don't really remember waking up, but thankfully I did! My family were told not to visit until the next day. I do remember a doctor visiting and telling the nurses to get me into a chair. But I'm not sure if that was the Saturday night or the Sunday morning.

The nurses let Peter know that I was awake and talking. He was amazed because we'd been told that normally patients are sedated for a few days after a heart transplant. My stay in ICU was fabulous, I had one on one care.

My bed was opposite the nurse's desk, so when Peter rang on the Sunday morning the nurses called to me and I remember waving. Peter, Diane and Debbie visited me that day. I was sat in the chair, but I just remember that I kept falling asleep. Not a very good host for my visitors, was I?!

I didn't eat very much to start with. But I loved Calippo ice lollies, so I had some of those; very refreshing!

I was on painkillers intravenously. The heart medication I was given made me feel really sick, so I often had anti-sickness drugs as well. The pain when moving to and from the bed was really bad.

I was given a towel which was wrapped up, to hold against my chest. It's good to have when you're trying to sit up or if you think you're going to cough. I still had a catheter but if I felt I needed to do more; the commode was brought to my bed. There was only 1 commode on the unit, apparently, so I couldn't leave it too late to ask for it.

I had 2 chest drains. The nurse checked the discharge regularly, and when the time was right she said she'd remove them. I was warned that it wasn't a nice procedure. They were around my stomach area, under my breasts. They were taken out one at a time, I was told to breathe in as they were being removed and then the nurse quickly inserted a stitch. The second one was done and then a dressing was put on. Like I say it wasn't nice, but was soon over.

I had lots of bed baths and round the clock painkillers. After a couple of days, it was time for the pacemaker I had to be disconnected. The wire, which was connected to my heart remained in place on the inside of my body. On the outside it was coiled up and a dressing was put over it. The wire was removed after a week or so when I was on the normal ward.

I stayed on ICU until the Thursday, so just over 4 days. The time spent there is dependent on how each patient recovers.

While on ICU I walked around with the assistance of a nurse, I marched on the spot. And I visited the toilet several times after the catheter was removed. We take so many things for granted, but just being able to go to the toilet on my own – not having to use a commode - was bliss. The nurses were amazing, but to be able to do things for yourself is so much better.

Peter visited me every day while I was on ICU. He must've been so tired, but it helped me so much.

When you leave ICU, depending on how you've recovered, you either go back to the Coronary Care Unit where the ratio of staff is higher per patient, or you go to a normal ward.

I was told that I was being transferred to a normal ward. This was great news as it meant I was progressing well, but also scary because up until now I'd had one on one care. I wondered if I'd cope. Peter came to visit on the Thursday to help me settle in and bring some of my belongings back. Again, I got a single room but this time it had its own bathroom – yay!

Life on the normal ward

The next morning, I was told I'd be going for a biopsy to check for any rejection of the new heart. I was told that when I got back, I'd need to stay in bed for at least an hour. So, I made sure that I went to the toilet just before we left. The porters came and wheeled me down. All went well, so I was taken back to the ward.

I had my gown and dressing gown on and lay on my bed, but all I could think about was needing the toilet and not being able to go. Eventually I called the nurse. She said I couldn't go but she'd bring a bed pan. I explained I'd never used one before. What a disaster it was! The nurse sat me on it and I stupidly put all my weight on it. How did I think that a little cardboard bowl could hold my weight!

I heard a pop but didn't realise the pan had split. I was blissfully weeing, not realising it was all in my bed. The bed was soaked, my clothes were soaked, so I had to get out of bed anyway while the nurse changed it. I really don't have a lot of luck with toilet actions, do I?!

By now I'd been in hospital about 6 weeks in total and I still hadn't been able to shower. My days consisted of getting up slowly, easing myself out of bed, having a wash etc. and then sitting in my chair awaiting breakfast. Blood tests were done, weight recorded, and blood pressure and temperature were all taken each morning. And the nurses would bring round my medication several times a day. I didn't know what I was taking or what each tablet was for, there were so many.

Soon it was time for me to self-medicate. A nurse from the transplant team came to teach me. I was given a little green book to record all my medications, and a pencil. Also, two plastic boxes that had 5 sections in each, with set times to put my tablets in. It was best to use a pencil in my book as my medication was constantly changed. The daily blood tests that I had determined my medication and how much of it I was on.

I was given so many packets of tablets, I had to get used to what each one was for, and the amount of each one I needed to take. The book had been filled in by the transplant team to start with and the nurse did a trial run with me, setting up the tablets in my boxes. I was doing ok, but then one of the tablets I hadn't realised was 20mg and I needed to take 40mg, so I needed to put 2 of them in my box. The nurse noticed that I'd only put 1 in and corrected it.

I'm glad I made the mistake while the nurse was there because it made me realise how on the ball I needed to be. I was on 12 different types of tablets, 5 times a day. From then on, I self-medicated every day at 8am, 10am, 2pm, 6pm & 10pm. A nurse from the ward would come in and check what I'd taken at those times, so she could mark it off on her system. The only thing I couldn't self-medicate was the blood thinning injection which was done in my stomach at 4pm every day. Every patient has this - it stops blood clots forming when you're not moving about so much.

I had lots of visitors still. Not every day, but then I was a long way from home. Jack and Tom would FaceTime me, which I loved. The doctors continued to visit daily, and also a physiotherapist. He gave me advice on what to do, to build up my strength. The main ward had distance markers on the wall. I needed to start small, and build up to walking the full length of the ward as often as I could.

He explained that there would be no physio staff working at the weekend, but there were exercise bikes on the ward that I could use. He said if I wanted to, I should ask a nurse to bring one into my room. On the Saturday I did just that. I was really proud of myself; I'd managed to do 5 minutes on the bike. I also started the ward walks.

Weekends were a lot quieter, which was nice. But on the Sunday morning before I got out of bed, I looked at Facebook. I started to read all the lovely comments off family and friends, from the week before, when I'd gone down for my operation. I couldn't stop crying, there were so many lovely comments. I'm not sure what the nurse thought who brought in my breakfast. I think it hit me then, exactly what I'd just been through. I ate my breakfast, got out of bed and kept myself occupied for the rest of the day.

Due to the medication I was on, I was also temporarily diabetic. A diabetic nurse visited me and gave me a blood testing machine so I could manage that for myself.

The time had come for me to have my pacemaker wire removed. It's a procedure a bit like the drain removals, so not nice but didn't take long.

I thought I'd finally be able to have a shower but, alas, not. The nurse said it was best to wait until the next day, so the dressing didn't get wet too soon. It was now over 7 weeks since I'd had a shower. As you can imagine, my hair looked gorgeous! Up until now I'd just been tying it up, without even running a brush through it. I'd always had really thick hair and it was quite long, so I hadn't had the energy to do it properly every day. I decided that afternoon to untie it and try and comb through it. I carefully ran my fingers through it at first. So much of it fell out. I didn't get too upset as I knew it was because I'd not done anything with it for so long.

The next day I was allowed to shower! It was amazing, the showers in the hospital automatically switched off after so long. I had the longest one ever - just kept switching it back on. I only had a couple more days in the hospital. On the Thursday – 12 days now since my transplant - the doctors visited and asked me if I wanted to go home.

Of course, I said yes. It would be scary, but it would be so lovely to be home. Some of my family were there when the doctors visited. They asked was it not too soon, but the doctors said it was my choice. They said I could recover just as well at home. I'd need to go back on the Monday, but I could spend the weekend at home. I then found out there was a final test that I needed to do, to prove I was fit enough. But if that went well, I'd be going home the next day. The test was to walk up and down a small flight of stairs, which I passed with flying colours!

Before I left, the transplant nurse came to have a chat with me and Peter. She brought lots of booklets which we went through, together. They gave details about what to look for, for signs of rejection / infection, and what I should and shouldn't do. Things like: I'm no longer to clean out our cats' litter tray, I need to really cover up in the sun. What I should no longer eat and when I should have a flu injection. I was also given my CRIB, which is a timeline of appointments and what will be done at each one, for the next year.

The first two appointments comprised of everything – blood tests, biopsy, chest x-ray, ECG and an echo test. The biopsy, I've explained how that's done earlier, is performed in the cold Cath Lab.

The chest x-ray was done straight after the biopsy. It's done to check that no damage had been done during the biopsy. I just had to stand at the x-ray machine, which was at chest height, and an x-ray was taken.

For the ECG test, wires were attached to my body using stickers. Under my chest, on my ankles, on my arms – about 10 in total. I had to lie on a bed, it didn't hurt and once everything was connected, I just had to relax while a reading was taken. I was then given a printout to give to the nurse.

The echo test is a scan of the heart. Cold jelly was used and a probe to scan over my heart. The nurse pressed on pretty hard and I had to lie on my side and stay in the same position for at least 10 minutes, which was quite tricky. The nurse shouted readings to another nurse sat at a desk. I didn't understand anything that was said, but occasionally I heard my heart beating.

At other appointments I just had to go for blood tests. One of the anti-rejection medications I'm on is Tacrolimus - TAC for short. I had to take this at 10am and 10pm, but it was really important that when I went to the hospital for blood tests, I remembered not to take the 10am dose until the test had been done.

Other things that were on my CRIB were suggested dates for contacting the DVLA about driving again, getting my eyes and teeth checked, returning to work and being fit to fly again. The last appointment was for the MOT which was set for 12 months after my transplant.

Initially the appointments were weekly, sometimes even twice a week. This continued for about 3 months, then they changed to fortnightly. After a further month they changed to monthly, the last monthly one being in December. The final one, 3 months later, was my MOT.

Time to go home!

So, Friday came, the day I could go home. I waited patiently for Peter and made sure I had enough medication. Everything was in place for me to leave. The ward was a long way from the hospital entrance and the car park, so a porter kindly took me in a wheelchair. After all, I'd not been walking very far in the last 8 weeks!

I got into the car. Peter had brought me a pillow to put in-between me and the seatbelt, to make the journey comfier for me. And, also, in case he had to hit the brakes suddenly. I was still very tender, and the 2 and a half hour journey was uncomfortable, but I couldn't wait to get home.

We arrived at about 7.30pm. I slowly got out of the car to see banners and balloons welcoming me home. It was so lovely, my boys were waiting for me. I'd been craving pizza, as the food in the hospital was lovely and obviously healthy, so pizza was never on the menu. As a treat we ordered a takeaway.

I sorted my tablets for the next day, then we headed off to bed. The last 8 weeks had taken it out of all of us. Even being in my own bed I didn't sleep that well, I had to lie on my back. I couldn't sleep on my side; it was too painful. I continued with the painkillers, but they wore off around 4am. So, I got up, had some more and made a brew. I then lay on the sofa with a blanket and dozed, until the rest of the family woke up. Getting out of bed was painful, a strange feeling at the top of my back. It felt as though my rib cage was really heavy and it would fall through. I had to get up very slowly.

The disturbed nights went on for a couple of weeks - I wasn't complaining, though.

Diane visited me on the Saturday, as she was flying off to Florida the next day with Cheryl and her family. And also, Jean and Peter's sister Samantha came. They'd come over from France again to visit me in hospital. They didn't realise I'd be discharged so soon. They were staying at a hotel in Birmingham, close to the hospital, so had to get a train to Manchester to come to visit me at home. I had to sit in a dining room chair as the sofa was far too soft, it was really uncomfortable. Tom made toasties for everyone. It was lovely.

Soon it was Monday, my first hospital visit. I got up at 5am and got ready slowly, and we left around 45 minutes later. I wore baggy clothes, as it was too uncomfortable to wear a bra, and I used my pillow again for the drive. We arrived just after 8am.

We slowly walked from the car park to the reception of the outpatient's department. I checked in, and was called to have my blood pressure and weight taken and my blood tests done. Then it was off for my biopsy. Because it was my first time, I didn't know where to go, or how far it was from the reception. A porter was called, who took me there in a wheelchair.

Peter and I sat in the waiting room, then a nurse came in and gave me a carrier bag to put my clothes in and a robe and socks to change into. She took me to the toilets to change.

Then it was off to the Cath Lab to have the biopsy done. I slowly climbed onto the table and was given a lovely blanket to keep me warm.

Everything seemed to go ok, I went back to the waiting room to collect Peter, then off we went for the chest x-ray.

Once this had been done, we went back to the reception to wait to be called for the other tests. I had my ECG and echo and then went to the toilets to get dressed. We then waited to see the transplant nurse. She asked if I had any problems and went through the medication I was on – checking that I had enough etc.

Next, we sat and waited to see the doctor. He checked the ECG and echo test results and asked how I was doing. I had chance to ask any questions I may've had. He explained that I'd receive a call at around teatime that day, with the results of the biopsy. They'd let me know if there was any rejection showing. If there was, there was a likelihood that I'd be admitted while they tweaked my medication and possibly put me on intravenous antibiotics.

He said I'd also get a call the next day, once they'd had the results of my blood tests back. On this call they'd tell me whether I needed to change the dosage of any medication, or stop taking any altogether.

In the early days my medication was changed regularly, so it was handy to have piece of paper and a pen ready to note the changes down. Then I'd update my green book. I'd also receive a letter a few days later, confirming what the changes were.

The next few days I just pottered around, trying to do what I could around the house. I couldn't bend down very well, even to feed the cats. I had to put my arms down to steady me. I was very slow when walking up and down stairs. And I couldn't reach up into the cupboard to get things like plates. It was painful to lift anything, and I didn't have the strength. I wasn't allowed to go out for 6 weeks, apart from the hospital appointments, so taking it easy was fine. I'd get up to see Tom off to school then doze on the sofa. I'd usually have a shower in the afternoon.

I did have to make an appointment with my GP to go through all the medications with him and get them on his system. The anti-rejection drugs were always given to me by the hospital, as they said they liked to make sure I was always given the same brand. But the rest of the medication I was told to get from my own GP.

Peter made the appointment and I stayed in the car until I was called. I had to be aware that I could pick up any infections very easily, so had to protect myself. Prescriptions weren't free for me, so it was beneficial to apply for a pre-paid prescription. The cost of this was £10.40 a month, a lot cheaper than paying for 12 different types of tablets each month.

As the days went on things did get easier, although I found I still couldn't have a bath. I didn't have the strength to be able to get down that low and sit down. So, I continued to have showers for a while.

My hair continued to fall out in large amounts which did upset me. It was getting really thin, but I really didn't want to have it cut short. The only bonus was that it dried very quickly. I tied it up loosely most days and ordered a shampoo which was recommended for hair loss.

The hospital visits continued, some of which were just to have my bloods taken. It was a long way to go but it didn't bother us. We were just grateful that I was being monitored so well. Peter continued to do the shopping, cooking and do most things round the house. I did what I could, e.g. he'd carry the washing upstairs and I'd put it on the maiden. We went for little walks around our close to build up my strength. I did feel very self-conscious and was worried about going out at first. We live at the bottom of a hill, so it was good to be able to reach the top! Soon we started going for longer walks every day and I had an exercise bike at home which I went on daily.

Hospital visits changed to fortnightly. A couple of my scheduled visits from the CRIB were cancelled, as they were just for blood tests and the doctors were really pleased with my progress. At one of the visits Peter asked about my old heart, if it had been checked. The doctor checked the records. Apparently, all the tests came back inconclusive, so no reason had been found as to why my heart had failed. It was probably due to the virus I'd had, it could've attacked my heart. But the doctor advised that Diane and Debbie should both go to their GP and request echo tests to be done, in case it was a genetic problem.

Soon, the 6 weeks passed so I was allowed to go out. It was lovely to be able to go to the supermarket again. I still couldn't drive, but that didn't matter. I also started to go for walks on my own, small at first then building up to really quite long ones. I was also able to carry a bit of shopping.

I received a letter inviting me to attend an exercise class. The first session was to assess me and then there was an 8-week course designed to build up my strength. I was the youngest one there, and the only one who'd had a heart transplant. Before the usual warm up that we all did, I had to pace the room to get my heart ready. And again, at the end of the class, walk slowly up and down to allow my heart to settle. I was very self-conscious until I built up the courage to speak to a few people and explain that the physios had told me to do this and why it was needed. At the end of my 8 weeks I was assessed again and was told I'd done really well.

I was asked about my diet and the exercise I did at home. We also discussed alcohol. I was told I could have a drink, a maximum of 8 units a week I think they said, but not to save them all up for, say, the weekend. I've had the odd glass of wine, or prosecco, on special occasions.

I continued with my fortnightly hospital visits. The doctors reduced my medication based on my blood test results. And because the steroids were being reduced, the amount of hair I lost reduced. I was so pleased. I was still on the diabetic medication, so had to test my blood regularly at home.

Peter and I celebrated our 23rd wedding anniversary. We went for a lovely Italian meal. I treated myself to a glass of prosecco!

We'd also booked a holiday in the UK. Just for a week. Before we knew it, it was time to go. I'd made sure I'd packed enough medication for well over a week, just in case of any problems. The break was lovely, but the hilly walks sometimes took their toll on me. I started getting a real pain in the back of my right leg. I didn't want it to ruin the holiday so I carried on, the best I could. But sometimes we had to cut our visits out short and go back to the log cabin. We had a lovely time overall. We met some friends on one of the days, who were staying in the same area. The week was over in no time and it was time to go home.

So now it was about 6 months since I got my new heart, and all in all I felt pretty well. Things had settled down with my leg and it was business as usual at home. My next appointment at the hospital was a couple of weeks away as they'd changed now to being monthly. But at my last hospital visit I'd asked the doctor about driving again. He agreed it would be fine, but that I needed to contact the DVLA first to get their approval.

I decided now was the time, so I gave them a call. I told them about the heart transplant and the diabetes. They said they'd send me some forms to fill in. As soon as I got them, I filled them in and sent them back. It didn't take long for them to get back to me saying I could keep my licence and was fine to drive again.

It was funny at first, but I soon got into the swing of driving again. But I only did very short journeys in the beginning.

I'd met with friends several times. Sometimes they'd come and visit me at home, other times I'd go into town to meet them. Each time I was really anxious about the visits. I felt like I'd lost my confidence, didn't really feel like 'me' anymore. My hair was really thin, my face quite fat. I knew I had so much to be grateful for, but it was still hard dealing with the changes. I remember thinking I'd never feel quite the same as I used to. And I wondered what my life would end up like.

A couple of times when I was out, but also sometimes at home, I experienced dizzy spells where the room spun very fast. I just had to stand still until it passed. I started to diarise when these happened and what I'd been doing prior to it happening. But there weren't any common elements.

The day came for my next hospital visit. Everything went well with the tests, or so I thought. Even when I saw the transplant nurse, she commented on how well I looked. I'd not seen this particular nurse in a while, so she could see a huge difference in me. It gave me a real boost. Next, we waited to see the doctor. We walked in and I was buzzing at what the nurse had just said, but the mood soon changed.

The doctor told me there was some bad news. The echo test had shown a problem. Something was flickering on the screen which he showed us.

He said it wasn't a one off because it was showing on every view that he'd looked at. There was something in my heart, he went on to say that it could be a blood clot, or it could be a tumour. But whatever it was had grown pretty quickly as it hadn't shown at my last appointment.

Whatever it was, needed to be removed. He said they would arrange further tests and started me on some blood thinning tablets. He said they would admit me once the tests had been arranged. We went home feeling quite disheartened. Everything had gone so well in the last 6 months; I'd had no rejection whatsoever. But it was Tom's birthday the next day, so we focused on that. We had a lovely day. Tom had an inset day before going back to school after the summer holidays, so we made the most of it.

The next day I drove Tom to school, I'd not done that in well over 7 months, so I was really pleased that things were getting back to how they used to be. Later that morning I received a call from the hospital. They'd decided it would be better to admit me as soon as they could, so the tests could be done quicker. They said as soon as they had a bed for me, they'd let me know. Peter had arrangements to go out with his friends that night.

At 4pm the hospital called again; they'd not managed to find me a bed so would try again the next day. Peter got ready to go out and I set off driving him. We'd only reached the top of our close when my phone rang again.

It was the hospital, saying a bed had become available and they wanted me to go in that night. We quickly turned around and Peter let his friends know that he couldn't make it.

Re-admitted

I got my case, which I'd had packed for the past few months just in case I'd ever had any rejection and needed to be re-admitted. I added a few extra bits to it and grabbed my tablets. We set off for the hospital. We arrived at about 8pm and I got myself settled. The room was a bit like a storeroom. It had just enough room for one bed and had storage cupboards along one side. Peter set off for the long journey home.

The next day the doctors visited me and explained they'd be doing several tests to try to find out what was in my heart. I moved rooms to a much bigger room, halfway down the ward. It was a single room, with its own bathroom. As I wasn't connected to any drips this time, I was able to shower every day.

My room overlooked the Helipad, so I got to see the helicopters arrive and leave. This was quite nice to watch, but then I remembered that it meant someone was seriously ill.

As the days went on, the tests began. The first test was, I think, called a trans-oesophageal echo. It involved putting a camera down my throat. I remember when the porter came for me, I didn't really know what the test was, which was probably a good thing as I didn't have time to worry about it. When I did realise what was going to happen, I did worry a bit, but the nurse explained that I would be given some medication to numb my throat and it would make me a bit drowsy. It wasn't a nice experience, but I think I was expecting it to be worse.

Another test I had while I was there was an MRI scan. I'd not had one before, but I knew you had to lie as still as possible. I lay on the bed and was given a headset as the machine is quite noisy. The bed moves you into the machine. I think I was in it for a good 20 – 30 minutes, and was constantly told what to do, e.g. breathe in, hold your breath, breathe normally.

The last test I had was a CT scan. I was taken down for the test but, when the nurse saw me, she said my blood tests had shown that my kidneys weren't working well enough for me to have the test. She said I needed to go back to the ward to have some fluids intravenously for a couple of hours. I was taken back to the ward for what turned out to be all day. Eventually at about 5pm I was taken back down for the test to be done. The CT scan is a bit like the MRI scan, but you're injected with some dye. I was warned before we started that at the point where the dye is injected, I'd feel like I'd wet myself. I did get a warm sensation down below, which was very weird.

I had visits every day from the doctors. Lots of them. They kept telling me that they'd never seen this before. They'd researched and couldn't find anything similar happen to a transplant patient. I'd been in hospital about 4 days, and the tests had shown whatever it was, was still there...but they'd not been able to determine what it was.

It was decided I should be started on blood thinning injections instead of the tablets I was taking. Apparently, it takes several days for the tablets to leave your system, whereas it's only 24 hours for the injection form, which was better for when they needed to operate. The doctors confirmed that I definitely needed surgery, but it wasn't decided if it would be open heart again or if it could be done as keyhole surgery.

I was told keyhole would be a quicker recovery time, but it wouldn't be as easy for the surgeons to perform – or get to the right place to remove whatever it was. Open heart surgery wouldn't be as complicated as my transplant but with all the scar tissue to get through, it could take just as long. I was keeping my fingers crossed for keyhole as Peter was supposed to be flying off to Turkey for a golfing holiday. We thought if it was done as keyhole, he may still be able to go.

Unfortunately, the decision was made for it to be open heart surgery, and it would go ahead the following Thursday. After a lot of discussions, Peter cancelled his trip. I had a week to wait. I continued with my routine - getting up, breakfast, shower, walk around the ward.

I was also allowed to go off the ward, l just had to let a nurse know before I went. It was lovely to be able to walk further and even go outside in the fresh air. I also had my word searches and my iPad, to stay updated on my soaps. The last visitors I had were on the Sunday.

The next 3 days would be long, but I knew the days after my operation would be tough for my family, so I didn't expect them to visit. I still had the great group chat I'd set up when I had my transplant, with all my lovely family and friends in it.

That kept me going, too. I had lot of visits from doctors, I was even asked if I would sign a form allowing photographs to be taken during the operation. The doctors were still amazed that it'd happened, and they'd spoken to other hospitals who - like them - had never seen it before.

Surgery number 2

Peter arranged for him and Tom to stay in a hotel on the Wednesday night. So, they could be at the hospital early on the Thursday morning. Jack had flown off to Benidorm the Saturday before so he couldn't be there, but he rang me on Wednesday night. Diane wasn't able to come as her echo test was arranged for the same day as my operation. Debbie came early on Thursday, so in my little room was me, Peter, Tom and Debbie all waiting patiently for me to be taken down to theatre.

We'd been told that I'd be going down early, but an emergency must've come in because it wasn't until about 2pm that the porters came for me. Like before, my family walked to the operating theatre with me. I said my goodbyes. It was just as hard as last time - we were all crying. I was wheeled into the pre-op area.

I was still crying, so the nurses tried to take my mind off what was about to happen. We talked about holidays and where I'd go if I won the lottery. I couldn't think – possibly New York. But all the places I'd thought about in the past - Maldives, Bahamas - seemed out of the question now with me having to stay out of the sun.

The mask was put on my face to send me to sleep, and I remember thinking it wasn't working – it didn't take this long last time. But it did work. The next time I woke up was a total surprise. I still don't believe how lucky I was. I was groggy so it was hard to take in, but I was told that the operation hadn't gone ahead.

They'd started by putting a camera down my throat, which is apparently routine so they can monitor what they're doing on the screen while they operate. Whatever I'd had in my heart had gone! Lots of additional doctors had been called into the operating theatre and they all confirmed there was nothing there.

I was shocked, but obviously very relieved. Peter, Tom and Debbie were brought in too, to be told. We were all so happy. By now it was about 7pm and I was taken to ICU. Apparently, my temperature was pretty low, so they wanted to settle me in as soon as possible. Debbie said her goodbyes and left quite quickly – it'd been a very long day! Peter and Tom stayed a bit longer, but then also left for the long journey home. It'd been a very strange day.

I stayed in ICU overnight. I felt bad as everyone else looked so poorly and I was so well. The next morning, I had breakfast and waited for a bed to become available on the ward. I messaged everyone to tell them the good news. No-one could believe it!

Later that morning I was told a bed was ready. I was taken back to the ward - the nurses were shocked to see me back. A doctor visited me, and I asked if I could go home. He said maybe, but wanted to check that I had enough of the blood thinning tablets, which I did. Later, when all the doctors did their rounds it was confirmed that I could go home. It was about lunchtime, so I called Peter who set off to pick me up. When he arrived, we just had to wait for the discharge papers to be completed.

We walked out of the hospital still not really believing what had happened in the past couple of weeks. Arriving back home was lovely. I unpacked my case and settled for the night.

I always have a case packed now with the basics, and I have a list in there of extra bits that I'd add if I was admitted again. Things like my phone charger and iPad etc. The things that make a hospital stay a little bit easier.

So, the past couple of weeks I'd been thinking I was going to be back to square one, after being opened up again. I thought I'd be in a lot of pain, have to stay in, unable to drive for a long time etc. But thankfully this wasn't the case. I was pretty much where I was two weeks ago, but because I'd not done a lot of exercise, I needed to build up my strength. I started my walks again and I used my exercise bike. But I also bought a second-hand treadmill so I could keep up with my exercise even when the weather wasn't good.

I had to attend an appointment with the Occupational Health Service. It'd been arranged by my employer. They assessed me to see if they thought I could go back to work. I was really anxious about the appointment, but Peter came with me.

Christmas was fast approaching so I was thinking a lot about that. Strangely I wasn't back at work so had plenty of time, but I couldn't motivate myself to actually buy anything. It felt like there was a lot of pressure this year to have a great Christmas as last year was so bad. And sometimes when you build something up, it can really disappoint. I didn't want that to happen.

I had a couple more hospital appointments. Everything went well – again, no rejection! Luckily as the weeks went on, I began to feel more Christmassy. We put our Christmas tree up the first weekend in December. I'd ordered a special angel decoration, with the date of my transplant engraved on it, so I gave that pride of place on the tree. And I took a moment to think about the lovely lady who gave me such a special gift.

I started crossing people off my list, meaning that I'd bought their present. And we went on a family meal in the Midlands. We met up with Debbie and her family and exchanged gifts, which was lovely. I went on my works' Christmas do. It was lovely to see everyone, but I was a little anxious about going with me not being back at work yet.

Christmas came round really fast. It was a lovely day. The turkey didn't quite cook as I'd planned, but the breast meat was cooked very well. A huge improvement on last year, I was actually able to eat it! Boxing Day was quieter than we'd planned. Cheryl and her family came, but Peter's dad and Shirley weren't well, which was such a shame.

My next hospital appointment was 30th December. We set off as usual at 5.45am. It was pitch black. I said to Peter that it'd be light soon.

He laughed and reminded me that sunrise wasn't until about 8.30am and we'd hopefully be at the hospital by then. We drove all the way in the dark - it felt like the middle of the night. There was very little traffic on the road, so we arrived early. We had a drink in the café before we checked in.

All the tests went well, and the call that night was again great news – no rejection! The hospital called the next day and the only change to my medication was to stop taking my diabetic medication. The diabetes was temporary, due to being on the steroids. My test results had shown that this was no longer needed, which was great news. So that was it for this year!

Tomorrow was New Year's Eve; we'd been invited to a family house party. It was a great evening and I even had a small glass of champagne at midnight.

We were all celebrating and hoping that the next year would be better than the last. I woke up feeling good about 2020.

The new year begun and was going well. We celebrated Peter's birthday in February. It was so much better than last year. We managed to go out, for a meal and then to the cinema. Much better than a trip to A&E!

My next hospital appointment was 9th March. This was my MOT. As far as I'm aware you have MOT's at the end of your 1st, 2nd and 3rd years. Biopsies are done at each one, but then unless you have any more problems that's it – no more biopsies!

We arrived at the hospital. I went for my biopsy and the doctor joked that he thought it was my 3rd MOT, he'd seen me so often. They all joked that I was a trouble causer because of the re-admittance in September.

When we went in to see the doctor at the end of our visit, he said that everything looked good on the echo test and ECG, but he was a little concerned about my kidneys. He was basing this on the last blood tests from December, because the results of today's tests wouldn't be available until the next day.

He said there were 3 options to consider. They all meant changing my medication, but 2 of the options could mean more risk of rejection. The 3rd had side effects that 1 in 4 people suffer with, so they usually have to change from that option. Whichever one we decided on, it'd be better to do it sooner rather than later, as damage to the kidneys can be irreversible if left too long. But it wasn't so severe that we couldn't wait a few months.

My next hospital appointment wouldn't be for 6 months, so I needed to make an appointment with my GP for 3 months later, to request a blood test to check my kidneys. To hear that from the doctor was upsetting, but I understood that I needed to take each day as it came, do what the doctors told me, eat a healthy diet and keep up with the exercise.

I went home and waited patiently for the call that night. It came through and again I had no rejection. I was buzzing!

So that's me, one year on. And what a year it's been! Every day is different now, I do worry about every twinge. And if I do too much, I wonder if I've done any damage to my new heart. I'm also not great with working things out in my head anymore. I'm not sure if this is due to the medications that I'm taking. Or just that I've not worked in over a year, so I'm out of practice. But I'm still here and staying positive!

Some may think it's strange that although I have a will, which I made many years ago. I've never felt the need to plan my funeral. I know it's probably a sensible thing to do. But I just want to be optimistic and not think about that.

Sometimes I want to forget about what's happened, because naturally whenever I meet people that's the first thing they ask/want to talk about. Which I know is lovely and obviously a major thing in my life, but without sounding ungrateful I just want to be 'me' again. The fit and healthy person whose life was pretty much planned.

I've felt like my life was on hold until a decision was made as to whether I'd go back to work or not. But I've kept busy and enjoyed spending lots of time with my family and friends. My employer has now offered me ill health retirement which I've taken. It's not how I'd planned my life, retiring this early. But I think it's the right thing to do.

It's time to say thank you.....

I can't thank my amazing donor enough. Without her I wouldn't be here. I also have to thank all my lovely family and friends as I'd never have got through the last year without them. I've received so many gifts and cards throughout the year that I'm so grateful for. When I reached my year's anniversary, some of my friends sent me a lovely scarf with hearts on it. And arranged to have my name engraved on the Heart of Steel which is located in Sheffield. I'll definitely be going to visit that soon.

We've met some great people at our hospital visits. One kind lady who approached us on one of our very first visits, had her transplant 17 years ago. A gentleman who'd got so ill, he'd defied all odds of surviving. But he was still here to tell the tale. Another gentleman had problems coming to terms with the fact that he had someone else's heart in his body. But I think speaking to other people has really helped him.

All these success stories, due to the amazing donors but also the fabulous doctors and nurses at the Queen Elizabeth Hospital. I can never thank them enough for what they've done for me. And of course to everyone who cared for me initially at Tameside Hospital. They managed to stabilise me so I was able to be transferred, ready for the rest of my transplant journey.

So, here's to many more years. I won't count my chickens as I've already had a year that I certainly wouldn't have done without my new heart. But I'm staying positive and looking after this special gift that I've been given.

Printed in Great Britain
by Amazon